SCATTERPLO

PREVIOUS WORKS

Coil
(1998, 2006, University of Alaska / Permafrost)
winner of the Midnight Sun Chapbook Contest

Tunic
(2013, speCt! books)

Twine
(2014, Bauhan Publishing)
winner of the May Sarton Poetry Prize

Compendium
(2017, Omnidawn Publishing, co-edited with Alan Soldofsky)

SCATTERPLOT

DAVID KOEHN

OMNIDAWN PUBLISHING
OAKLAND, CALIFORNA
2020

Cover art:
Tucker Nichols, *Untitled (PA1903)*, 2019
10" x 8", paint on panel

Cover typeface: Avenir LT Std
Interior typeface: Adobe Caslon Pro & Avenir LT Std

Cover & interior design by Cassandra Smith

Printed in the United States
by Books International, Dulles, Virginia
On 55# Glatfelter B19 Antique
Acid Free Archival Quality Recycled Paper

Library of Congress Cataloging-in-Publication Data

Names: Koehn, David, 1968- author.
Title: Scatterplot / David Koehn.
Description: Oakland, California : Omnidawn Publishing, 2020.
Identifiers: LCCN 2019049086 | ISBN 9781632430779 (trade paperback)
Subjects: LCGFT: Poetry.
Classification: LCC PS3611.O3626 S29 2020 | DDC 811/.6--dc23
LC record available at https://lccn.loc.gov/2019049086

Published by Omnidawn Publishing, Oakland, California
www.omnidawn.com (510) 237-5472   (800) 792-4957
10 9 8 7 6 5 4 3 2 1
ISBN: 978-1-63243-077-9

ACKNOWLEDGMENTS:

"Morning Meditation Busted Sonnet Sequence Failure 19," *Borderlands*

"The Day We Translated Catullus 8 in Mr. Nemesh's Latin Class," *Cider Press Review*

"From Symphosius: Word Problems #38" & "Types of Angels," *Compose*

"Yosemite Lostness Fable," *Columbia Poetry Review*

"Delta 3: The Jewel-shaped Dorsal Shield—Doesn't Just Look Like Danger," *East Bay Review*

"Ode to a Broken Typewriter Found While Hiking with My Son," *FIVE:2:ONE*

"Delta 15: The Definition of a Circle in a World without Geometry," *Aquifer: The Florida Review*

"Delta 17: Slough Water Never so Clear as Flow Tide in November," *Free State Review*

"Delta 10: The Green Plastic Flyswatter on the End Table Looks Like a Bug," *Gargoyle*

"$10,000 Pyramid Sonnet," *Glass*

"In Limbo at the Millennium," *Greensboro Review*

"Delta 1: What We Called Pickleweed Was Everywhere" & "Delta 19: If You Were Given a Self-driving Car What Would You Do with It?" *Green Briar Review*

"Delta 20: Crossing the Bridge to Tassajara Trail," *Hotel Amerika*

"The Shadow Thief," *Interim*

"Delta 5: September 7th the Day After Reading Antin's john cage is still cagey I See Waterweed Everywhere," & "Delta 6: At the Corner Of Byron Highway & Camino Diablo There Is a Stoplight," *The Laurel Review*

"Hocus Pocus," "Abracadabra," & "Delta 11: We've Heard Rumors the Water Hyacinth Was So Thick," *Letters*

"Delta 14: On Our Last Walk Past the Edge of the Neighborhood I Noticed a Man Patching His Fence," *Mayday*

"Poem to be Cut into Confetti," and "Portrait of the Artist as a Playlist Sonnet," *Mary*

"Delta 2: At Night We Walk & Talk To the Far Edge Of The Subdivision," *Juxtaprose / Midnight Oil*

"Field of View," *Mudlark*

"Essay on Granite," *North American Review*

"Noose," *Pinch*

"I Dream I Am Walking the Streets of Some Unknown Metropolis…" *Prairie Schooner*

"I Left Out That Part…" *Shadowgraph*

"This Year I," "Superman Battles Cthulu Under the Watchful Eye of the Zap Gun," & "In a Family Room Of a House Where a Three-Year-Old Is Raising His Parents," *Smartish Pace*

"What Amanda's Looks Say," *Sparkle & Blink | Quiet Lightning*

"Delta 7: Walking Over Here Today I Asked My Son, Bay, What Poem I Should Read," *Talking Book*

"Supernova," *TAB*

"Delta 13: After We Walked the Sand Ending in the San Francisco Cliff Sides," *VisitantLit*

DELTA 1: WHAT WE CALLED PICKLEWEED WAS EVERYWHERE

Swampfire, glasswort, and what we call pickleweed:
Between our teeth the briny coruscation
Confuses the tongue with complexity.
Across the water, near lines of storage sheds,
A man in black socks, canvas shorts, and t-shirt
Fished for something. Bay and I walked
The slough's ragged edge. Above the keyboard
I grab a gnat out of the air. The empire's delta ebbs
And what looked like waste
Flowed toward Central Slough. A muskrat
Plopped in the water, surfaced, and we noted
Webbed hands, the thin tail, and then the dust
Mote of brown murk. Bay tells me rats
Hold their breath up to 30 minutes
But I don't know if he means muskrats or not.
When everything shines what does not glitter glows.
The eyes of a scallop run the entire
Equator of their body. We raise an eyebrow
At cornfields, and grass fields, cherry orchards,
And architectural levees of the floodplain.
The quail root in and out of the field grass
And pearl-grey lizards scurry into the crisping brush.
A cliff of gnats steeple over the water.
Songbirds ascend, chitter, fall silent,
And swoop. Aside the bent gate
Once locked shut now open enough
To discourage property damage yet closed
To keep vehicles out: there, a couch, a couch
That had a color once but for the weathering,
Takes on the tint of dirt. Who brings discomfort
With such intention to the shade of this tree?
I thought of how my son from early on expressed
His clear understanding that he was formerly
A creature of some otherworldly place

Where he was one of many of himself,
A self that was also self-separate
From the many and he saw who his mother
And father would be and chose a life
He would have and have to give up that other world...
Holger Czukay in "Shikako Maru Ten" asks
"Are you, are you, are you, are you, are you, are you?"
As advised for aesthetic purposes, I leave out
Two geese, their necks straining above the spikerush,
How they stared us down. Let's not mention
The two purple jet skis as they leap and buzz
Away from the docks at the end of the cay.
Let's not mention the worn RV propped aside
The port-a-potty not far down the northwest
Riverbank. Here I need to note that I know
I am going to die, and death has made the rounds
At our house. Suicides in the solar system. Friends.
Girls our daughters' ages—one hung from rope.
The other jumped from a bridge. Insert lovers
Knee deep in blue beneath a palm, nuclear
Reactor in the distance. They have no place
Here. I do not want to mention the shadow
They cast. And now I am upset with my son
For spending hundreds of dollars on app
Purchases on his iPad and I yell and his mother yells
And I wonder if he understands at 8
Having lost some of that shine from the other
World, roughed up with the patina and rust
That this world puts on us until our frame
Rots away—the old VW Bus
Can no longer be fixed—is this the world
He chose? Did he not see that the promise
Was just temptation and now he
Has no choice but to endure? A bumblebee
Thumps against his forehead. Hush now.
Teeth abrade the weed, and the scene takes root.
All down the slough, everything going to seed.

SCATTERPLOT: I DREAM I WALK THE STREETS OF AN UNKNOWN METROPOLIS WITH ANTHONY BOURDAIN

Loosely asleep, after the Father's Day my kids
Don't call me, I dream of meeting Anthony Bourdain.
I am on a bus to a bus to another bus to a departure.

"This is no accident," he says. "Ditch your adverb.
I made some calls, and I have to say I am pretty
Disappointed. I mean based on what I was told

You were less American Gothic, I was expecting conversation
About the redistribution of wealth in post-Utopian autocracies
Or a drunken brawl atop the tallest building in the city

Where we get arrested for putting at risk the only,
If relatively average, daughter of the Sultan."
What can I say? I was stumbling around the aisles of a dream.

Bourdain and I ascend toward silvery transits.
He looks me over with what I think must be disdain.
"Look, the hero, the anti-hero, the priest, the doubter,

They all depend on self-righteousness. Avoid that."
He steps away. I wave and descend the stairs
Away from him. Now aboard, he grabs the handset

From the engineer and over the intercom says,
"Dude, that Dean Yeagle T-Shirt is for someone
Fifteen years younger. What can I say?

I kind of think you're a doofus." *Who is Dean Yeagle?*
Beep. Beep. Beep. This is the sound of this poem
Backing up. I hear a piece of the house singing.

What's the rule? Never write about a dream. Never.
I guess some people are just born to be assholes.

.

DELTA 2: AT NIGHT WE WALK & TALK TO THE FAR EDGE OF THE SUBDIVISION

The wild yarrow surprises no one. The hard-to-hear palm trees talk about the
man-made
Lake behind the "No Fishing No Swimming No Boating" sign. The cat,
underneath the mailbox,
Ignores me. You'll need to know this: my partner and the mother of my child
has been married
To her husband for 27 years. At the end of Miramar street where planned
houses
Have not been built yet, where teenagers park to do what teenagers do when
they can, a path
Walks away from the neighborhood. Who has not known the exclusive
altitude dolor ascends
To, the distance they fall. Night fishing is illegal. The moonlight reflects off the
rod stems:
Mindfulness a convenience death brings with lawn service. The soon
To be dead contract to do death's work. The barking of Rottweilers
Occupy most of the local backyards—where watering the lawn comes with
complicity
The need for the elected HOA requires. Cats? When I move I leave them
behind.
I do not want to be in the business of the profound. I wrote this poem for four
people:
Bay, Rusty, Scott, and you. You will be interrupted three times while reading
this poem.
My son asks, "What is your favorite crustacean?" Pauses, inspects, knowing my
shoulders will open.
He says, "Mine is the mantis shrimp, also called a rainbow shrimp, a fierce
predator that sees
Color not in three color receptor types, red, green, blue like us. Sixteen. The
rainbow shrimp
Sees in sixteen colors." He pauses for effect. Eyes wide, his mouth drops open.
His hands at the end of the twigs of his arms open towards me as if learning
to catch

14

A ball. He wants the idea to land and work its magic into our conversation.

The way grounds turn water into coffee. The way steam softens asparagus. The
way sun

Repeatedly pulls the monkey plant in the corner of the bedroom toward the
window.

The way resentment looks like it might have been present in a Schiele painting
but has leaked

Away to be replaced by something more congruent, something in the same
family

As anger. "It also has two claws that shoot out of its face into prey. The claws
faster

Than a bullet." Bay's mom walks into the room, she taps away on her phone,
she never lifts

Her head, announces she is taking her kids to the parking lot of the church in
Byron

To drop them off with her husband. "Answering Machine" by The
Replacements

Plays on Spotify. Buried fears linger like the carpet's wet dog. Unpleasant,

Noticeable at first, noticeable to folks who visit the house, but an aroma

That eventually fades into things. "Sonoluminescence," Bay says. "The rainbow
shrimp

Swishes its legs so fast that the result are these bursts of light, tiny photon
torpedos."

He pauses, "These photons demolish their prey." Every guitar string strum

Sounds different than the one before. Strumming sounds the same by
musician

As much as by model of guitar. You and I cannot play a string on the same
guitar

The same way. Not really. And I think of my son walking along the street of
the abridged

subdivision back from the wreckage of the Central Slough and the few sparse
trees and what

We call pickleweed amok over the wet spring earth. We call it pickleweed
because we

Have not found it in a reference book but see its tangled lines as the defining
shape

Of where we live and feel the need to give it a name. The rainbow shrimp sees
in those thirteen
Additional photoreceptors. How does the imagination imagine colors
That can't be seen? I suppose he reaches into some marsupial pocket available
To him—mine grown shut from lack of use. A photo box found at an
Atherton estate sale,
In the bottom, a set of negatives. He holds them to the light and they trigger
Not only what the ceiling light shows in the frame but what the image on the
negative
Would have been or could have been. I used to see things this way—in sepia
desire escapes,
Colors the lawn, the blue Ford Maverick rusting in the driveway. Aquariums
Don't keep rainbow shrimp. They dismember their colleagues. Alone they take
on the aquarium glass.
I'm told the Monterey Bay Aquarium tried to keep one. At night in the dark,
the watchman
Would hear the tap against the glass. He would turn his light on the tank and
thwack, thwack, thwack, thwack, thwack.
You have written about wild yarrow before. Drank yarrow tea. A white
bandage dress walks
Into the center of the living room. "What do you think?" she asks. "Will this
work for tonight?"
Off in the dark of the cul-de-sac, car windows steam over, beyond them a
rocky point.

SCATTERPLOT: THIS POEM WILL HAVE 452 WORDS…

Our living room
Includes your books, her books,
His pictures, their books, my books, their pictures,
An oversized red couch and a large Sony TV. "How much
Does this cost,
Daddy, how much do books
Cost?" All of the flashcards passing for currency
In your hands. "Okay, thank you for the books!" a guitar, an easel,
Blinds, a toy
Chest, bookshelves (implied?). "Space may
Look empty but is full of stuff, debris
…the solar wind included…astronauts can see
It as if you are awake
With your eyes
Shut." In <u>The Codex Hierosolymitanus</u>,
There are only two ways, death and life.
My four-year-old son hands me four flashcards:
Iguanodon, Torosaurus,
Indian rhinoceros, roseate spoonbill.
The two sets,
To him, seem self-evident.
Visit four rocky planets orbiting the inner
Solar system. Visit four fogged planets arcing in the outer solar system.
Fe, the word.
The library's Byron, Darwin, Kant,
Kepler, Campbell composed of, essentially, the same stuff.
The modern didache, taught to me by a high priest remote behind bifocals,
Revealed how rules
Have their roots in art.
Consider the relation between Katie Morgan and Morgan
Freeman. Cockatoo, Tuojiangosauraus. The kitchen's icemaker bumps around
    like a clumsy grandfather looking
For a pair
Of wingtips in his closet.

"Come check out my library." And this, I
Suppose, is where optimism bias proposes the librarian drives a yellow
Caterpillar
Along the ice
Roads of Barrow, Alaska. Green
Bananas yellow while holding too-ripe peaches in lusty
Fingers and buckets of junk show why dinosaur toys feed on this grappling
With death—with
What was terrifying, strange, reptilian.
I'd say clawed and fanged but the Siberian
Tiger provides evidence of the other. God told me you become less dinosaur
But your actualization
Resembles pizza. Cut cheddar's sharp
Milkiness tinged with sliced soppressata's oily bite charges
The chilled air and returns Easter when uncle Doug lustily kissed aunt Mary
On the steps
Between the second and third floor
Out back of Uncle Joe's, just off James.
Childhood recollection collecting childhood recollection. Every sneeze. But
    gas planets don't have solid
Cores. They hold
Shape, remain pressurized, a liquid
Mystery at the center: see Jupiter. Fortunately time
Eventually solves every scientific problem. Every mystery is a scientific
    mystery. Styracosaurus, Komodo
Dragon, prairie dog,
Allosaurus. Chunks of asteroid brought
Water to earth. "Look at all my money.
I don't want to go to bed yet." Flashcards. "When the clock's hand
Is at 6
You're done." The large clock
Hangs on the wall in a Venn diagram
Shadow of a light above. "Look daddy, my movie room, here is popcorn."
T. rex folds
His tail forward to better
Fit his velour seat. The previews start now.

SCATTERPLOT: IN A FAMILY ROOM OF A HOUSE WHERE A THREE-YEAR-OLD IS RAISING HIS PARENTS

There is no mistaking the smell of piss and shit.

There is no mistaking our essence rolled up in a disposable diaper.

Yeah, yeah, yeah. I know. The windows are the shattered glass of delusion.

The hallways reek of mashed peas with diced idealism.

I remember saying, "How could they…" And "I would never…"

And "Some people…" because I was young, smart and better than I am now.

Relative to the sun, the earth spins clockwise.

The body ache wrinkles with an anxiety unfamiliar to my earlier self.

In this house, with the garbage can full of shitty diapers,

The floor plots a minefield of die-cast and dinosaurs and wooden blocks.

With your mother's ashes on the mantle, a future mortgage, and a future
    college tuition you cannot afford,

You turn off the TV and you will find your way to the sleeping child's room.

You will curse his graceful slumber, the ease of the breathing.

Yet, and here is the expected turn my younger self could have predicted,

I do not fault my youthful, drunken assessment.

The morning in New Orleans when I woke from a blackout with a tattoo on
    my back?

This makes that me more credible not less.

Relative to the sun, the earth spins clockwise.

Yet, and here is another anticipated turn, you are not happy and you are not
    fulfilled

And when you make love to that boy or girl you are not making love to her or
    him, not yet.

In this house, the kitchen island a raft of dirty dishes, is where you begin.

Though winter, spring's pavilion and the rock garden of your childhood will
    take shape within you.

There is no mistaking the smell of piss and shit, but tonight it is love's
    aphrodisiac.

And now, maybe, maybe for the first time, maybe the last time, ever,

You will be the breath of everything that dreams.

DELTA 3: THE JEWEL-SHAPED DORSAL SHIELD—DOESN'T JUST LOOK LIKE DANGER

A ladder blew off the back of a contractor's pick up
Onto southbound Vasco Road, a one-lane byway.
The A topples between the lines forming the sound a mouth
Makes when reaction voices its only option.
Quail dart and yaw, two thoughts depart then one
Into a mess of burdock. According to gravity,
The universe contains 2 trillion galaxies. Two doves
Flush but stop winging as they arc peripherally
Then back into view just down the slough where they alight on schist.
Tall sandbur and bank thistle slide then grab against t-shirt
And jeans. Grasses going to seed abrade the breeze. If ignored
Resentment filtered the view, low visibility
Would be the forecast. Abrade? My favorite new product?
24 karat rolling papers. I should be grateful.
But am exasperated with trying to count to ten.
A black-legged tick hitches a ride. A field hawk glances
Over its left shoulder, tacks into angled flight arcing
Along the path where the slough touches burnt foxtail. Worn trails
Of tractor tires reveal evidence of summer
Frozen by heat. A blue heron keeps switching sides
Of the slough. "Is there too much 'nature' paraded in this poem?"
Asks Scott. Insert backtrack. I walk through the quagmire,
C-sharp, because I like to walk off the last argument.
D-flat, each spat a tax for avoiding the unspoken.
G. The inevitable moments before a car crash
Provide a kind of clarity—to live one's life again
Or less likely to not. "You are a terrible mother."
I say, "If you don't like it here, feel free to leave." I say,
"You have the right to ask when you're not married to someone
Else." Listen to a game of ping pong while a music box
Plays in the background. Days later shiny piles
Of window glass still star the northbound shoulder. I'm not thinking
About the birds, or risks like rattlesnakes. My youngest son

Talks as he brushes salted butter on his sourdough bread.
"Did you know there is such a thing as a tongue-eating louse?"
I suppose I raised my eyebrows enough to encourage
Him, "Cymothoa exigua, a parasite
That eats a fish's tongue and then pretends to be its tongue
Taking part in eating whatever the fish eats." What silences
What? Back at home, the air has lost ionization.
My tongue not my own. "There are no leaks in the external shell…"
Says Gerty in *Moon*, the voice, Kevin Spacey. Sam Rockwell
Plays the stressed astronaut locked into a continuum
Of selves. I pull my t-shirt over my head, feel the tick
Cross my chest. On the tip of my finger, curved front pincers:
The alien capitulum; the jewel-shaped dorsal
Shield—it doesn't just look like danger. When the leg's cleat
Caromed off the side door into oncoming traffic, I
Was grateful the ladder was not flying into my lane.

SCATTERPLOT: I-LEFT-OUT-THAT-PART BUSTED SONNET TANKA FOR AMANDA

I did not include the span of grey deck, ~~the hypothermic aspens shivering in~~
    ~~the cool dawn of the attendees assumed~~
~~Disdain of the well off. I left out the thrum of Subarus and Tahoes arriving~~
    ~~and landing, departing and ascending~~
In the interstitial gap below the comic's wish ~~to be taken more seriously aside~~
    ~~the profound's wish they could crack~~
~~A joke.~~ I neglected to mention the new spans ~~of fresh-rubbed lodgepole fence~~
    ~~so bright in their gaps bordering the valley's golf course,~~
The Olympic rings off in the distance above a tie-dye backdrop, Harryette
    seated at a little table, a plastic
Geraniumed tablecloth covering a self, ~~though I have no self yet, that I do not~~
    ~~want to parody.~~ Did I mention
The caribou, the cigarettes, the hot redheads, the broken sliding glass door, the
    dysfunctional hot tub on the back porch: I
Left out those parts too. The way the ceiling fans hyphenate the ill-lit common
    space with Newton's rings, the $N\lambda = 2nt$
$\times \cos\Phi$ of intermittent morality—a concept you are aware I have some flexible
    ideas about
As in what might or might not constitute a breach of the social—well pretty
    much any – contract, yes, I forgot to tell you
About the creak of the chairs and how that sound, repeated everywhere I sat,
    ~~how the wood of chair backs jointing into their seats,~~
Reminds me, even now, of our gradual whispering, our hardened nipples
    brushing each other's chests with signal, and how our
Own creaking frame soon has traveled on its way, and the secret we thought
    we were hiding bangs our voices against our walls, trebled
Over the sudden rush of traffic, for no wind can shake an aspen so furiously
    lest the root structures themselves give way,
And even if a moose or bear or Stephen Colbert walked through the screen
    door and club-footed into the kitchen ~~to chill out~~
~~With a whiskey sour,~~ we, in all likelihood, would not hear anything,
O, O, no I told no one, I cut that part out too.

SCATTERPLOT: WHAT AMANDA'S LOOKS SAY…

"She was not one for emptying her face of expression."
—J.D. Salinger, Franny and Zooey

This red sock?

Shutup. Oh my god. You have to be kidding me.

That was my self-deprecating humor pointing out your paradigm intending to
   box me into a deterministic response to your mis-judgment.

That's right. "I wanna rock and roll all night…"

Huh? Yeah, right.

The roll of my eyes is not really rolling my eyes in the conventional sense of
   rolling one's eyes to show exasperation or contempt but rather a roll of my
   eyes meant to communicate a combination of exhaustion, drunkenness on
   pleasure, and complete connectedness.

Asshole.

That was the artist's attempt to create the illusion of dimensional space created
   by perspective.

Help yourself.

Your idea of normal and my idea of normal are clearly not the same.

Much gratitude for this gesture. I know you think this means I will now have
   sex with you but you are sadly mistaken.

Much gratitude for this gesture. I know you think this means I will now have
   sex with you but…I was going to have sex with you anyway.

Folding, folding, folding, folding, folding.

If you only knew what my sister said to me today!

Oh really? You did what?

You smell like rotting oranges.

The picture makes no sense, Pilate's servant holds a water pitcher, hovering,
   with nowhere to stand. Pilate's hands will never be washed clean.

Back away from the sink.

I was reading Janus by Koestler and in the chapter "Physics and Metaphysics"
   considering Jung's essay "Synchronicity: an Acausal Connecting Principle"
   I noticed a quote you'd previously highlighted "…the seemingly
   accidental meeting of two unrelated causal chains in a coincidental event

which appears both highly improbable and highly significant…" and it
occurred to me you should consult a therapist.

When you say that, you better mean it.

These are your instructions: _____.

I understand, like no one else, that you come from no place and belong to no
one and every room you walk into, you know no one and no one knows
you and that you are the empty space they fill with that person who has
not been there before who is not one of them. And I know you love this
about yourself, otherwise this would be tragic but I know how I mean to
you and how you want to mean to mean to me.

Look, a piece of the moon.

Yesterday walking Columbus past City Lights, we walked over a sewer cap,
"Neenah Foundry, Neenah, Wisconsin." You tell the story about all you
have to do is look in the sewer to know where you came from.

Keep it to yourself.

We are out of milk.

We are out of squeaking floors and horse flies.

We are out of clothes rusting, coughing, landlines, ramen, doors that won't
lock, lack of plumbing, roadlessness, distance.

We are out of here.

We are out of blue eggs.

This is embarrassing.

We are not done. In front of the mirror.

We are expanding our understanding into new territory.

I said, "Yes, I will get my passport taken care of…" but now that I have said
this you know this means "No, I won't."

He holds the violin under his chin without using his hands.

I know you see me standing here, stop rolling your dirty socks together.

I am sleeping. I am dreaming. It is a good dream.

Wasps! Yellow jackets! Dragonflies! Fireflies! Swallows! Wild Turkeys!

I remember. Your mother's cancer spread to her brain. You were at her bedside.
She rose like a bobber popping to the surface of a pond. Her first words?
"Did the Packers win?"

I've missed you. We are out of milk.

Like Scott said, break their fucking hearts.

DELTA 5: SEPTEMBER 7TH THE DAY AFTER READING ANTIN'S john cage uncaged is still cagey, WATERWEED EVERYWHERE

On today's walk up the slough, I was not with me, there was no muskrat,
No cowbirds, no geese in the distant field. The sun owned last month.
Unbeknownst to me the daughter I bought a car for on her graduation
From college has fallen in love with a friend of her mother. Also unknown
To me, my girlfriend has set up a pied-a-terre at her ex-husband's.
Bay wears loose sevens. I bought him eights and they fell to his knees.
The water in the slough usually green and clouded with plankton flows
Clean through the Brazilian waterweed, the spooky tentacles urging
The fish past, filling the trough with the deception that this passage
Is also shallow. I'm not supposed to watch football. Like smoking
Its appeal should be passé and its harm a fundamental truth to intelligent
Sensibilities. Perhaps I don't have intelligent sensibilities.
The season opener features the Chiefs versus the Patriots. My performance
Review from work advised me I sometimes think things are good enough
When they are not. I don't count as precisely as I should. I count
People in when they are out. "Kareem Hunt, third-round pick out of Toledo,
Never fumbled away the football in close to 700 carries. He fumbled
On his first carry in the NFL." On the couch next to me is the sky-blue
Soft cover of David Antin's john cage uncaged is still cagey.
I find myself thinking about dry-farmed tomatoes, their flavor
A throwback to pre-industrial food chain. They remind me of tomatoes
Picked off the vine near Siena, rubbed clean on my t-shirt,
And bitten into. Flavor fills the mouth with a surge that registers
As intellectual surprise, as if a great idea had just occurred to me,
But there was no idea there, just tomato.
At the edge of the slough where I expect to find fishermen,
Enough already, nothing is fucking sacred. That is what props up
Disbelief in scientific truth; there is however my dream of us.
I wait expecting to see a bass surface from the fingers of the waterweed.
I wait expecting to see a speedboat rush past, hurrying from where to where
I don't know. I wait for the doors to the storage garages across the field
To open. That is my problem, isn't it. My part of expectation is avoidance

Of what is really happening. What is really happening?
On the album Occult Architecture, Moon Duo's "Seven"
Makes melody the lyric, you know, the effect that made drugs fun.
Four practice-range golf balls litter a ditch aside a cornfield.
I left the TV on, a commercial for the premiere of the 10th season
Of Parts Unknown. What is really happening is that I have not
Been listening to my son, he has been saying "I love walking in nature,
It makes me feel good, I don't know, it just always has." On the wall
In the living room of our house is a 2' x 2' Sterling & Noble wall clock.
Time rules that room, the ever-quivering second-hand signaling.
Antin noted of composition as process, that "the whole piece is divided
Into six sections stanzas or cantos and each section opens
With the same opening line: 'This is a lecture on composition which is
        indeterminate with respect to its performance.'"
My daughter doesn't love me or more precisely she doesn't love me enough.
The bookmark in the Antin has a shopping list written in black
Felt tip pen with six items: Water, Chips,
Ice Cream, Paper Towels, Milk, Potatoes.
What is really happening? The runs of light slice the leafless olive
Into fragments. I too, boys, take a dim view of comparisons. We plan
To frame the office and the hallway with astragal to match the doors
Throughout the house. Chippewa Falls, Wisconsin, 5th grade,
We played football in my neighbor's yard. I dove on the ground
To recover a fumble, before I could pull the football back to my body, Jeff,
Jealous that I was "dating" Sally, landed on my arm and snapped the ulna.
The ulna was yanked up into my bicep by the strength of the tendon.
Florida suffers, and suffers, Irma makes a mess of her garden. Irma
Crushes the pumpkins with her heel. She pulls wax beans out at the root.
In film noir, is there a truer character ever invented than Verbal Kint?
When Kint limps up the street and, through the art of blocking, straightens
Up and walks evenly and keenly into a defined future, who does not cringe
And see how life is like Kint, telling the story we need to hear from details
In our midst. The lie that gives and gives, until appeased, we let it slip away
Without penalty despite the con. Keyser Soze does not exist, I live in fear
Of him. In the high heat, coyotes lie dead on the side of the road
From here to San Francisco. This is an incredibly thin tracking device.
In this heat, animals change their ways, will go to any length to find water.

SCATTERPLOT: $10,000 PYRAMID SONNET

Things remembered from staying home sick from school:
Smoked cranberries crushed under a rolling pin,
An unexpected phone call from your sister,
The desire for women who are afraid of goldfish. Things disease inspires:
A day the neighbor girl snapped her arm jumping onto the island;
The rock garden's labyrinth, the not-so-secret room where they took you;
The crayfish in a blue bucket;
The RCA's convex screen and the underlying tube, the allowed for distortions,
  the antenna;
Her laugh when Jamie Farr says "memories, peas, potatoes, the name of my
  sitcom,"
& " the undiluted self recognizing its own inability to discern self-interest
  from sadness..."
Things to be mashed up:
Buying a bag of dried cherries;
The sense of smell, the taste of taste, the sound of hearing, sight seen, feeling
  felt;
What the unpracticed guitar considers on the other side of joy.
Things not porch swings: an unplugged TV's loveliness, a decade of one night
  stands.
Things this body has forgotten and cannot parse from the red carrot:
The feeling of the touch of her fingertips on my cheek pointing the way.

SCATTERPLOT: ABRACADABRA

Lay a set of spoons on the table in front of the audience.
Watch the daughter crawl into the hospital bed
With her now dead mother. The word
On a seven-year-old tongue catches:
Not the ruse of hocus pocus or the sleight of hand of presto.
Show the audience the spoon in your left hand,
Bend the spoon held in the right.
The daughter had been waiting bedside for death to arrive –
Which is a kind of waiting for her mother, the resident, to depart.
Say the word out loud, *abracadabra*
Just as she did that day. The room encircled
By Hope Mills, North Carolina.
The eye loves the roots of the tree
Grounded in Aramaic. The ranch
Home, white, with gray shutters, and three street-facing windows,
The largest one set within the frame of the front porch
Lined with small evergreens: the grey lizards, angled and opium-eyed, bask
In the sun and wait for capture. Millais' *Ophelia* drifting on the river,
By her left knee look for a purple flower,
Just left of there, a spoon. Hold the spoon up in line with the audience
And shake it. I showed our mother my first magic trick,
Some part of me wanted to be Uri Geller –
To change the world with the power of my mind.
When I bent the spoon, she seemed astonished,
Her face lit up with what I assume must have been mock surprise.
No incantation brings her oddly stilted "Für Elise" back,
No trick allows us to feel the way we do with the living while they live.
Turn the spoon sideways to show the bend.

SCATTERPLOT: HOCUS POCUS

Pick a card any card, the ace of spades, the tarot's magician.

What the hand knows the eye can never know. Shuffle the cards all you like.

As a child, watching *The Cabinet of Dr. Caligari* changed my life:

The murderous somnambulist let loose on us by the insane hypnotist.

I dreamt that the affection I felt was legerdemain.

Fan all the cards to show the shuffled array, the random order of things.

On the back page of the September 11th, 1908 Nashua Telegraph

There is an ad for Clark Stanley's Snake Oil Liniment

Where "the body is a machine of flesh."

I did not dream of ten bassoon players arcing the air with a B flat.

The card trick always looks like magic until the trick is revealed.

The orbs would float between us, hovering, absorbing our attention.

They would drop from the air into a copper bowl I could not quite put my
    arms around.

Cut the deck anywhere. There they would disappear.

While he performed a boy became uncomfortable in his skin.

A woman stopped loving her children.

I became thirsty and walked to the spring where I drank

And no matter how long or how hard I pulled the water into my throat I
    could not stop my thirst.

The mock Latin that invoked our attention was nothing but a distraction from
    a distraction.

The body's repositioning of what the body senses

Just after surprise. There is a deck of cards in the drawer, the fourth card, the 7
    of clubs, has your name on it.

The snake oil salesman selling snake oil that contains no snake oil has won.

We have given ourselves over to the illusionist

Rather than the magician, to the vacancy's porchlight at the end of the street

Rather than the dragon in the stars, to the dream of something rotten

Over the love of knowledge or our children. Our lovers fall to their death.

DELTA 6: AT THE CORNER OF BYRON HIGHWAY & CAMINO DIABLO THERE IS A STOPLIGHT

My mind was a hidden camera before there were hidden cameras.
I stitch you into me, the homemade quilt only understands
Scraps of scrap. I have wanted to write about the Gainesville murders
For some time now. In the '90s a serial killer stalked the campus.
We were advised to live our lives as normally as possible.
Please ignore the alligator in your swimming pool.
Next. Remove the "r" from a friend and you get a fiend.
The pinch in the cheeks when teeth clamp down on gum wrapper—
The way nostrils pinch, I am what happens
At the red light of a crossroads when no cars approach from the left,
No cars come from the right. The roads, empty:
The staggering telephone poles carrying callers away faster
Than you can imagine their stories. Train tracks measuring the transect
Of the fields: an arbitrary column of paper cutout and pasted across the valley;
And off at the edge between Mt Diablo and where you sit, a ranch with most
    of its Arabians
Tucked away in their stalls under their blankets and in their blinders.
What happens on Craigslist when you want to sell your liver.
A Contra Costa County Marine Patrol Sheriff's boat sank today.
What happens when a woman you thought attractive becomes a man,
Who you still think of as a beautiful woman. You remember the one time
He hugged you after you bought her *On Violence* by Hannah Arendt,
His breasts pressed up against you, fondly, and you thought:
"Action without a name, a who attached to it, is meaningless."
Mosquitoes in Walnut Creek tested positive for West Nile Virus.
This exposition, architecturally speaking, frames space
For decompression of assumptions written between the ballpoint
Pen labeled Palmer House and the idea of measurement, meters,
Centimeter, and hectares. What are the properties that give you to me?
You own what you own. I am not trying to explain anything.
I am what happens before the artist covers the canvas in paint,
A background to the charcoal pedestal under the Marengo-shaded pot
Growing the fruit tree with the colored-paper tangerines. A cut out

Pasted on the brushed branches.

My partner calls the house a cave. Insists on keeping all the blinds closed.

There are horror stories about what happens when someone runs a red light.

There are no stories about sitting at the red light when no one is around until
   it changes.

She complains that the dog barks whenever she eats. Feeds it her dinner.

Cooking dinner requires her recipe for yours. Cleans up the dish you haven't
   used yet.

You snore, you fart, you don't pay the cleaning lady enough.

You need a shave, that shirt is passé, and you don't spend enough time

With your kid because you are always at work.

Murderabilia is not therapy. The dog will not stop barking.

You can touch the floor of every body of water. There is patio music, and a
   gunmetal bowl

Full of multi-colored marbles, and a teal pool float, and the alligator.

The plastic lime green flyswatter looks a bit like a bug:

Acrylic and house paint on canvas. This is an active homicide investigation.

Today, my son and I were walking around the block, and he wanted to talk

About a story he had "heard" (read: saw on YouTube) about an old briefcase

Found in the woods years after thrown there. He wanted

To know if I had ever heard of such a thing. Wondered if something

Like that could ever not be found. The improbability that the person

Would not have been missed, that an evil-doer had succeeded,

At least for as long as that briefcase was hidden. He could not recall

Where this had occurred, what state, or who had told this story.

But here we are walking along the edge of the development

Out along the berm, engineered floodplain just beyond the rise.

Somehow I had failed him, I could not shield him from the knowledge

That someone could dismember a body, place it in a briefcase, and hide

It in the woods. I wanted to tell him no evil stays hidden forever,

I wanted to tell him the truth always comes to light. Wanted to play back

All the Catholic school aphorisms I was programmed to say

At times like these. I remembered learning the magic

Of Strunk and White's Elements of Style and the sudden structural sanctity

Of the colon: a thing, a different thing clarified, and another

Thing of sufficient detail to place a finer grained understanding

Of the original in the mind of the reader. "Use a colon after an independent

Clause to introduce a list of particulars, an appositive, an amplification,
Or an illustrative quotation." Friend, do not stick that colon
After a verb. Two AA batteries power the remote control.
In everything there is a school of fish: horsefly season throughout the house,
Filing an extension for your taxes, the queen of wands. We lived down a dirt
    road
In a cinder-block three bedroom. As struggling graduate students
That was all we could afford. The sandy road, the occasional rattlesnake,
The tropical palms, the ever-wet air. Wendy wanted to fuck
But I told her "no." She was pretty offended. Bay just strolled
Into my office with his Batman ears over his Ninja mask.
In my room, drunk or stoned, I
Took flight from my body, felt forced out. Listen, Danny Rolling's heavy feet
In the sand and pine needles. He walks the windows of the house, thinking
    about who
Is behind the blinds. One person? Three? Man? Woman?
What if we had been women: sisal, manila, cotton?
I see him from the perspective of the crow on a nearby wire.
He was not cautious, he was interested, thoughtful like a taxi driver
Looking up side streets thinking about the fastest route from here to midtown.
There is no way to keep the presidency out of this poem. Or anything.
Look out the nearest window. The kind of things always goes away.
My partner did say something about taking a trip with her dad.
Their relationship
Is better than ever. She loves spending time with him now.

FROM CATULLUS: FOURTEEN ERASURES FROM THE LATIN OF THE FIRST THREE LINES OF CARMEN 48 BASED ON REBECCA RESINKSI'S ASSIGNMENT TO ERASE THE LAST THREE LINES OF CARMEN 48

moss, tules, basalt

most quiet

sets set seas sea

oculus enters

me too to sense in a us, a beast

melt slot, sentient use, amber cent

losten is a tribe

toss liquids etc…

solve sin, re-base recent

lost lists, labs

so close is is mass areas

it lost us, lensed me

little as a request

loss as a request

DELTA 7: WALKING OVER HERE TODAY I ASKED MY SON, BAY, WHAT POEM I SHOULD READ FIRST

The first thing I notice? Your blue shoes.
Soundtrack of *Teen Titans Go* too loud on the upstairs TV,
The lanyards on the hinge, cordlessness: I choke on everything
These days. We walk and talk. Let me hold this up. I drink
Lemon water because I'm tired of sugar, tired of everything
I put in my body bringing death closer. When Bay turned three
He noticed the lemon tree first. How limbs underlined window sills,
Took stage center in the neighbor's yard. If lemons had cosmology
The meaning of things in relief would be the source.
Somewhere along the way someone convinced me that lemon water
Changes the body's alkalinity.
If you read this aloud, this will take seven minutes.
I am not certain this is the best way to spend your next seven minutes.
"What is your favorite kind of coyote?
Of lizard? Of seal? Of crustacean?" On our walks we see things.
Wow, 1 a.m.. Time is a loose pair of slacks.
As I write this the skyscraper
In the background oversees the woman in overalls
Folding laundry. While sitting on my couch. I noticed your t-shirt,
Not royal blue,
A decal of a golden pig the size of your fist.
I eat dried lemon rind to erase the bad taste
From your mouth. Every real estate TV show opens—
A strip of film cut from Koyaanisqatsi. Koyaanisqatsi, the movie, yes? No?
I'm almost certain the first time I watched Koyaanisqatsi
I was tripping. I'm not sure where this is going,
Bear with me for a moment.
Not every room I walk into contains a pair of blue shoes. But this one does.
The gray pot seems either too far away
Or too close to contain the brown branches. The yellow
Flowers with apple-red centers seem apart from the stems—
Seem assembled pieces rather than a whole. Yet, from afar
The eye gathers background green-blue into sky
And places the heliot

Into mind and sets perennial thoughts adrift. Underneath pinkish paint
Of the body there is another painting, covered over, a texture
The brush strokes suggest, let me point this out, this and this and this.
The lettering on the pig, cursive, but I can't quite make it out.
The scribbled branches of orbital lemon lean over the backyard fence
Like a many-eyed giant. I am mentally ill,
I was raised in mental health institutions.
This makes self-diagnosis tricky.
Live karaoke in small dark bars, when mostly empty, is both horrific
And heartbreaking. There is no wild left, there is no wilderness either.
That's not true.
My son has a dime store toy,
The loss in the words "dime store" matter. The toy skull,
The off-white one associates to Halloween, with nonsensical stitches
For lips and a delta for a nose, when I squeeze it, oversized
Alien eyes, yellow corneas, black pupils, pop.
Here, I have the toy, here. Let me show you.
Eyes pop out of the skull, like a crab's eyes,
Sink back. The toy feigns surprise and provides surprise,
And comes with the requisite "Choking Hazard."
Chirm of the ice maker like the sound of the train in the distance,
Like the smell of coffee in the morning, contain the foreground—
What is always a minute away.
Time fails. Too tight of a fit tonight.
Any work when backlit is only a frame. No matter, thank you.
Bay pointed out "Why does a skull have eyes?" Don't mind me,
Next year I am going to erase the Book of Spectacles.
This year the 100 Riddles of Symphosius. Here's to your perfect cup.
Lemonade's last stand says the podium to your chair.
I write, "Standing here I am embarrassed by your attention,"
I have no use for language
That describes life as it looks to me. My ideas mismatch.
So I resort to stealing Rodins and drowning them in the San Joaquin.
In the foreground, a dark blue drum set,
A variation on gray plays a solo. Meringue, meringue, meringue.
To repeat the word meringue until the world loses meaning:
I have no choice but to love you.

SCATTERPLOT: SYMPHOSIUS WORD PROBLEMS #38

One coxswain coaxes ten rowers
On two boats, his breath
Directs both. I am part of a long drive, my early sound
That of the paddler, the latter a snake's echo. Affection teaches us
The art of war, to pursue the retreating and ambush
The attacker. If Donald divorced and Chelsea
Married Donald and Melania married Hillary
And Pence killed Bill. My son speaks, my daughter
Marries, my wife lives in the white space
Between me and others, and I
Am the distance between. The everything
Plus the monsters we populate hell with
Created the panther. My father feared me as a girl.
The dead are not dead. The dead are here, now,
Occupying the space between where you
Are and where your body is. The man typing
Is dead. The man watching the dead type
Is not. The fig trees of the island bleed
Plant blood called Byzantium. Where grit
Resides in the mill of the chest,
When you remove the silent "e"
A stag appears. The funny thing about a can of pickled herring.
Because olive trees, if you watch them
Long enough, kneel down and pick up
Their fruit. I am the funny thing about incest.
Sound, the answer is sound, the answer is
What is a sound, but an inlet, the drowsy cove
Where waves from the ocean lap against the shore.
The idea of sisters giving birth to each other.
Only virginity is postmodern, the snowy
Flowering of the date palm repeats the starry
White asterisks like so many questions.
Nothing stops lucid dreams or the black plague.

DELTA 10: THE GREEN PLASTIC FLYSWATTER ON THE END
TABLE LOOKS LIKE A BUG

Down Vasco just past the peak off to the west
A stand of windmills guard the edge of the contour
Where grass meets the cirrocumulus clouds—there
A valley oak, the bulb of canopy an assortment of synapses,
Forms its thought: a series of self-describing APIs.

After the game, I drive home alone because we take two cars
Everywhere we go as a precaution.
There are no right answers, only answers that move the conversation
Forward, and if you don't believe that, there are wrong ones.

In the restroom, on a white radish-shaped sconce, the green-gray,
Black and red housefly waits to do work. Somewhere near there
A woman sets up her Valley of the Dolls. Her dollhouse
Overlooks the view of the most fashionable in the favored nation.
"I make the poem of evil also, I commemorate that part also…"

At night when I walk the sidewalk to the ball field, streetlights
Give enough space for night sky to show stars. I wish I knew
More about constellations, the Chinese name of Orion
Or the Russian nomenclature for Ursa Minor. I remember

My friend Dave, from college, I was his friend, likely
His only friend, the first person I met where I could see
An internal world different than mine and vast in a way
I only saw glimpses of. He was tall, 6'6" and maybe 145 lbs?
Not even his afro could hide the skeleton wanting to walk out of his body.

He would walk, here and there and everywhere, and when he felt
The need he would stop by the library and he would chat
With me about the Collatz Conjecture or the hairy ball theorem.
The first, a function that when applied reduces any positive integer

To one. The second, a proof, that no function can produce
A flawless sphere. He was gay, he may not have known that yet.
He may still not know that. Bay, my son, on one of our walks,
Explained axolotls to me as one of the few amphibians
That never become truly amphibious, choosing to stay aquatic

For the entirety of their lives. As if they prefer
To never see the world outside of water, the dangers unwarranted.
Spoiler alert. In Les Incendies pure math operates
As a framing device for the strange series of seemingly impossible

Occurrences leading to Marwan's torturer and rapist being her son
And father to his own brother and sister. The triptych fails
The off-white surrounding the grey lithograph of a peregrine's feather.
[Look up. Insert a description of the first object you see.]
Salt or sugar in water before boiling corn? Either. Never arsenic.

I don't have a truth, you don't have a truth: we have both seen
Unbreakable truths broken with the glance from your mother,
My eldest son's second full-length feature film premiered last month.
The desire of the lover you desire, an unexpected death.

This is a good thing: the way the guitar in Deer Tick's
"Twenty Miles" clutters and declutters the vocals, the way
The green painting of 10,000 tiny brush strokes, each dabbed
On like the Chinese character for bird, makes flight less difficult.
I don't have time to explain. I don't have to explain time.

Let me explain: the dime store guitar I bought
To learn to play sits in the corner
Glistening with a universe of dust.
Dust is composed mostly of human skin.

The men who teased Dave when he'd walk by could only tolerate
Being ignored for so long. When next I saw him, his face
Was barely recognizable, and the scarring never went away.

And now for the hypothesis: the ingredients of what holds.
Should I describe it? Do I need to? Isn't it just enough to allude to it?

The orbital bone over his left eye had been shattered.
There were something like 100 stitches that ran from just left
Of his chin up the crease through both his lips, through his left nostril
Between his eyes and into and through part of his scalp.

Don't mind me I am rewriting the <u>Book of Spectacles</u>
As a periodic table of consequences. The day I discover
You are Dorian Gray, I discover the children of trick questions.
Something changed in him, something departed and left a space
I could feel but not identify. What left him, the edges

Of the wound left a hole the body can't repair.
I never feel so alone as when I am home. And sometimes I remember
A hay field, now a walking path paved as a series
Of S's, when Bay, my youngest, told me his favorite amphibian was the axolotl.

He described them as "a hairless cat if it were an amphibian."
Or what "the skeleton of a catfish would look like
If fish had exoskeletons." He said
They can regenerate "any part of their body. Any part.
And not just arms, but over time, even organs and parts of their brains."

He paused. Looked at me, said "even a part of their heart."

SCATTERPLOT: TYPES OF ANGELS

Pay no attention to the small box in the corner,
This angel misunderstands other angels.
This angel sees the world in only one dimension.
Imagination is a distance from the seen world
And therefore subject, at a minimum, to delta time.
The straight angel cannot imagine you
Or anything else, but consequently, you cannot imagine the straight angel.
Supplementary angels add up to the love you deserve which is not always the
    love you desire.
Angels that rust and trust. Angels in the negative space.
The light of their works will be the end of ownership of people,
The end of marriage, the end of inheritance. They allow you the illegal
    blueberry
And you stay free. All that is right in the world, and therefore impossible,
Can be seen in the sad-faced green eyes of the complementary angel.
When two people intersect, their opposition gives rise to vertical angels.
No star upstages these eyes. No rise goes unmet with wet heavens.
No embrace sums up the result.
When crimson angels
Become vertical the poorly evolved affections of our DNA swing towards a
    true north congruent
With the sensual truth of a bassoon's ungodliness.
The dove wings of the smallest acute angel close
And fold and draw shut without end:
The aperture of the smallest acute angel and nothingness, one.
The lipomata angel pickpockets thieves —
Pinches thumb and pointer together on both hands just inches from the eyes.
Squints to investigate your Mediterranean coronas.
Tells you where you have not been.

SCATTERPLOT: 5
AN ERASURE OF A PAGE FROM ARTHUR CONAN DOYLE'S
SIGN OF THE FOUR; FROM FOUR, A COLLABORATIVE
PROJECT WITH REBECCA RESINSKI

narrow

footstep

lithotype

unclaimed

DELTA 11: WE'VE HEARD RUMORS THE WATER HYACINTH...

You can walk on it. I tried to, to say I did.
What joy we take in her amusement of her amusement
Of my friends. On tonight's walk, the wind drove in a heavy load
Of skunk, we imagined a whole family sashaying
Their way among the light brown skeletons
Of the new homes, the maze of studs and joists
Oversized star maps, not-so-transparent transparencies.
Almost too late we noticed two stray dogs
In our return path, one brown, the other tan, one a lab
The other a Rottweiler mix. They meant no harm
But in the dark, unexpected as aliens, they make us rethink
The difference between safety and incurvature.
The tinnitus of the house where I sometimes live, the emptiness
Has the timbre of a madrigal, the movement of Reubens' red;
Has what's left after Judith slaying Holofernes (Holofernes
Fighting off the maid). No, Anthony, I am not referencing your post
On Artemisia Gentileschi, (You know, Artemisia Gentileschi.)
But Klimt. The sound of the dog's claws scratch the glass.
The Hannah Nicole winery sets aside the plow
During harvest season. I do. Sleep offers a foreshortened
100 ounces of gold flake in a cereal bowl. If desire
For what I am not was a history, a fistful of sea lettuce,
Slake for a detrital echo of the waves, would be
The origin story. My story does not resemble the world ascribed
To me: my mother? Gay. My cousins? Black. My nieces,
Taiwanese. My CEO, a woman. My orientation? Beyond
LGBTQ. My abusers, women. My daughter's sister? Inupiaq.
My oldest son? The son of another man. My youngest son?
The only white boy in his class.
Decades ago, boarding a plane for return to Barrow, Alaska
My oldest son noticed a woman holding a bundled child
In her arms. Its pinkish, almost-blue face a smoothness
In the rubble of the blankets. He said, "Dad, why is that baby
So white?" In Inupiaq

There is a belief that all things sing, everything has a song.
No stone, no caribou, no door has the same song.
In a rare moment of camaraderie one of the women in town
Gave me an Inupiaq nickname, the word for gnat, kirgaviatchauraq.
Today, the TV tells me we have the Texans versus the Chiefs.
The drag of an old razor over 3-day stubble. The cardboard
Box's reaction to the packing tape torn off its back.
Taint me with the imperial. Bad Brains,
"House of Suffering" plays in the background.
The line? "…I gotta let some joy in…" There must be a Zen
Koan about a peach orchard, where the owner refused to pay
The laborer for picking too many peaches. Easy Street
Is a real street in an imaginary town, or is it an imaginary street
In a real town? An open-side down glass jar wrapped
In gray paper sits atop a red brick's vertical parallelogram
Beneath the Sumi ink drawing of a chevron's version
Of a butterfly bush. The idea of Amanda is not Amanda.
The indecision about what to do with old birthday cards
Lingers. The teenage daughter whines. The dog whines.
The only thing never-ending is discontent. The Texan cheerleaders
Wear white spandex shorts and blue shirts: to notice
Is to put myself on notice. I noticed your pink shirt.
"Oh No," oh no, not another "Oh no!" I didn't.
Everyone here knows the sound,
The refrigerator's tight-lipped suction uncupped from the frame,
And closed, a drawer opened, or a jug shuffled and closed and opened and
     closed again.
Then the tink of the silver in the sunset
Yellow bowl. What we remember begins with cows on the ridge
Of the saddle, the edge of the ocean crashing into the continent
Just past their nose, and the queen palms
Sultry in their entertaining haberdashery, bowing
Toward Highway One and car after car of applause.

SCATTERPLOT: AMANDA'S SUPERNOVA

At age, the Crab Nebula,
Tugs on the Milky Way,
Tests the theory. I say,

"Something, something, something."
You smile that smile, the moon
Oblivious to its observation.

Far waves of supernova
Birth new stars. Astraeus,
Earth star mushroom,

Beneath our bedroom window
Collecting dew under their birth.
The audiologist inserts the aid:

A new iatrogenic
Enhancement. You look about,
Because that is what we do

When we hear music
Inside of our heads. Too-loud
Voices clank. The naugahyde

Squeaks. Fabrics rustle,
Cotton whispers. In the distance
You detect children and an air

Conditioner's thrum. The receptionist's
Voice, her radio, the music
From another room. Has it tuned

In a local radio station?
"Tempted by the fruit…"
Take a breath, disinfectant.

The doctor inserts an otoscope's
Empty black funnel
Into your ear. Later,

After evening's crickets
Alert you to their hiding.
Bloch's Siemens on Cheops

Shot lightning from his hands,
He imagined, like the pharaohs.
Science masquerading as divinity,

We decided. My "something, something,
Something," your labyrinth.

SCATTERPLOT: POEM TO BE CUT INTO CONFETTI

ticker tape	parade	of	language	,
what	the	gothic	Lowell	might
have	desired	.	recurrent	streams
of	the	voice	,	marbled
into	counterfeit	wind	,	vibrator
preferred	65%	of	the	time
over	the	real	thing	.
red	dye	number	5	preferred
over	chrysanthemum	in	every	market
study	,	MSG	enhanced	kimchee
outsells	MSG-free	2	to	1
and	organic	lettuce	is	100
times	more	likely	to	infect
the	human	body	with	giardia
than	industrially	cultivated	verdure	,
without	latex	condoms	sex	would
be	almost	extinct	,	but
massage	parlors	would	see	an
even	greater	expansion	in	proliferation
.	when	the	soldiers	return
from	Iraq	why	won't	an

electric	car	await	them	?
what	percent	of	mothers	of
U.S.	soldiers	are	from	the
upper	or	middle	class	?
make	a	draft	mandatory	,
go	national	service	!	eliminate
inheritance	and	in	one	generation
re-distribute	wealth	in	this	nation
.	motor	voters	unite	.
eliminate	victimless	crime	.	incorporate
your	family	,	be	born
into	equity	.	Eliot	would
never	create	a	form	undeserving
of	its	content	,	what
world	have	you	written	today
?	Trumped	grammars	kill	.

SCATTERPLOT: THE DAY WE TRANSLATED CATULLUS 8 IN MR NEMESH'S LATIN CLASS

Lily, there were crows in the field. I remember.

Lily lived next door, let me drive her IROC Z Camaro to the prom.

Lily told me my mother told her she would never have quit smoking if my
father hadn't insisted.

Lily told me about Luckys she would share with my mother. On

Lily's back porch, eating pie, chocolate cream,

Lily told me she didn't love her husband, Ron. Sometimes after school, leaving
the slightly unkempt Catholic schoolboys behind, I walked a row of
cornfield to

Lily's door.

Lily, there were crows in the field. I remember.

Lily's house, other than the lacquer of cigarettes and tanning oil, mirrored
ours. I secretly thought of her, invited her to me, reposed in

Lily's smoke. I caught my mother kissing

Lily, the day we read "Catullus 8" in Latin class.

Lily, there were crows in the field. I remember.

Lily, no spectrogram can detect the call of human grief from a crow's mimicry

And cannot see in a face the difference between pleasure and dismay.

DELTA 13: AFTER WE WALKED THE SAND ENDING IN THE SAN FRANCISCO CLIFF SIDES

If you are not in a hurry, I will make a pot of coffee for you.
The clipped bag of Lion oversees a sizeable green bowl of blackish
Brown. The tip of the tongue pecks at a grain,
Releases the beany mud into the pool under the tongue.
The riptides pull at the coast speaking in the tongues
Oceans speak. The gulls rip their way through the lift
And account for the folk sitting in their cars
—looking over us to what the sun might do, hoping it will do
What it has done for generations before us. Dampened
Air from a distance weathers the storm, and my son's face
Squints into the fogginess for something unknowable.
No one listens to Self's cover of "What a Fool Believes"
Playing on the car radio of the empty red Datsun, open
Windows surrendered to passersby. The blue suit jacket
With the teal and persimmon-tree print hangs in an ex's closet.
What else hangs there? A year from now Trump will be president,
I will not have foreseen it. "Look at these sand dollars,"
Says Bay, "We are gonna be sand rich." Between the parking
Lot and the shotgun homes, modernized
To some next world cleanliness, the telephone wires,
Swinging from poles off square from the seismically
Shifted street, contour the drawing of the eave of house and cypress.
A year from today I will take a Lyft so far from where I live
I can never return. That day, my girlfriend will have been married
To her husband for 27 years. Near Altamont Pass an abandoned golf
Course goes to seed. What were the greens are now rounded patches
Of golden monkey-flower, as if they were the circular footprint
Of the nearby windmills telling and retelling their alien riddles.
Stephen Colbert's right ear rests two inches higher
Than on his left. This is a beautiful thing.
If someone tells you they love you, at what moment do the words
Stop holding their meaning? Pain is the mustard.
When the boxes in the garage remain unpacked a decade later?

When you have lived together since before Obama
But the lease is in your name? Notice
Not a single picture of you and her on the wall,
On any shelf, not pinned to the fridge, not in a purse
Or wallet, just a child. Not just. A child.
The orange tent with the red-brown flaps anchored to the moonscape
Hosts a small fire, we count seven logs engulfed in flame.
Where wet sand shifts to ebb's gray-green
And slides into the next wave's moon, a woman in a red sweater
Pulled up to her elbows and too short canvas shorts, walks
An Australian shepherd toward a surfboard nosing a surfer
Into the set. I often think of addiction, of tan throw pillows
And children yelping at unpinned donkeys
Just beyond the red fence's belief about neighbors and criminals.
Look through your fist on your left hand with your right eye open
And left eye closed, pinch the thumb on the left hand
With your thumb and forefinger in your right and pull them apart, run in
        place.
"What I have to tell you cannot wait" is my favorite line
From Season 5 of Ray Donovan. I occasionally stutter now. No ceviche
Better than "Butterfish. Tamarind peanut marinade. Cucumber.
Lotus chips. Sambal aioli. Soy." The aroma of a fresh pot of coffee
Threatens the air with the opposite of the beginning
Of clay in the root of petrichor. The latest feed? "Celebrities
And their pets." In the wash, a Dungeness, ruby and pocked
With what must be certainty, moves away from me as I close
In. I see the scarab sinking into the tide pool, deep enough to eye me
To remain beyond my reach.
I wire money everywhere. Let's buy an apartment in your Toronto.

SCATTERPLOT: From FIELD OF VIEW

§

        Skin's wing, wing, wing, wing:
    Mosquito, honeybee, cardinal, ginger.
                      3600 wild mouflon roam Kahuku ranch.
            Two Color has new shoes.
      The gate is open.

    A wild mouflon sheep's 26" horns curve, descend
       A derivative of fiddlehead,
                Fiddlehead, arc of Archimedes
          Uncoils a fern's shade.
      4:15's flatbed races down the road
Carrying what comes before sun's brief set:
    Evening's francolins, the trades, chatter.
                Can every line carry the whole tune?

    There is no radio for any rat not eaten by a mongoose.

§

Skin's   wing,   wing,   wing,   wing:
I   forget   tallness. What   has   no   predators?
How   is   a soul   not   a batholith?
Sail,   current,   lift,   trail:
Two   stones   in a kukui   grove   sink.
Candlenut,   hollowed   shell,   bowl.   Flame.

Passion fruit   shorn   of   its seedy   pulp.
What   wobbles the newborn   lamb?
A spoon   stuck in   frozen   coconut milk.
Ghost   flames: side   flash,   hood   spread;
The details   only   visible   from the right   angle.
A small brown   lizard,   slick as a tongue, slides   under the foundation.
The tallest ohia tree,   gnarled roots exposed,   draped in dodder.

§
Skin's wing, wing, wing, wing:

The screech of two mongoose quarreling.

Gobble of the wild turkey, chicks call, call.
When the fence line disappears,
Peahen, peacock, bedded down, flushed.
Crown of the peabird, the rut of tire tracks in soft earth.
All night
Psilocybin mushrooms ride the back of a cowpie.
Morning's francolins court, preen, bluster, settle.
Two Color looks colossal in the pre-dawn glow.
The dove's tail angled up, down,
Out for balance on the thinnest of wires.

§
Skin's wing, wing, wing, wing:
The memory of a memory, the forgotten walking stick
Leans against the wall.
Two Color lips a fist full of grass.
The tiger moth's octagonal
Eye turns to keep me in view.
Though lost, I am held. What part of mother is moth?
The horse in the horse is white or brown?
The bird in the bird is flight or song?
The poem in the poem is hog or god?
Hog god, hogfish, hog grass, hog—
The slant of roof fills the catchment.

Another honeycreeper finds another corolla.
Lemons ripen on the lemon tree.

§
Skin's wing, wing, wing, wing:

A white-tipped ocean collapses on a black sand beach.
Echoed birdbone tapping in burnt kukui nut and sugarcane juice.
The map's legend, serial seamounts, stepped ridge, islands.
Minutes rollover. Sibilant ant hill.
The timing belt on a wooden workbench.
Mango halved, coffee bean ground, night's moth
Wide as my hand framed by the screen.
100 words for rain.
The skylight's Sumi ink, the tephra spray of night.

Windswept paint on a decayed canvas.
Extract the pigment of any place, any moment at any time:
Plant leaf, dirt, urine: dry to powder, grind. Volcano black.

§
Skin's wing, wing, wing, wing:
Two Color grazes, the cock crows.
The dried seed pods seed the decanter.
The plantation's cracked macadamia nut. The gate's open mouth.

The shadow line approaches my window.
Rats and cats busy themselves with morning's arrival.
In the shade of the mountain, Two Color eyes the sun
Creeping over the fence. Checks her empty feed bucket.

A pile of basalt points out the log between the studio doors.
The pasture's 50 fence posts carrying 4 lines of wire.
Yellow death, a dying leaf. Indian yellow
Supposedly distilled from the urine of cows overfed mango leaves.
On the porch, afternoon rains' white eye greens.

§

The forgotten walking stick leans
Against the wall.

Two Color has herself a new yellow bridle.
A bamboo stand wet with the air of goats.

§

Skin's wing, wing,
Half a station wagon,
Bamboo pops in
Hums as I walk,
My skin electric
Alert, on my arms
I turn toward
Aware, awake
As from peak to pivot
I am joined
All the branches.
The nettles,
Each twig shivers,
With the slight
Leaping from the surface

wing, wing:
swamped in field grass.
the breeze and wind
hums as I walk, hums
with the buzz, hair
like a horse's startled mane.
a common Ironwood Pine,
to a vibration of its shape
in no wind,
to

loop and settle—
ecstatic
gesture of particles
of gravity's pool.

§
Skin's wing, wing, wing, wing:
Pointillism's idea of the tree in the sun's cinema.
Track perception's sense of an oscillating sprig of light.

A ray's chord plucked—
The tree's fir lit with yellow and black,
Every stem, every nettle, every V, buzzes.

Arthur, can I use the word dazzle?
A cone of fluttering wings.
A vibrato of resonance:
A swarm of short period events, then a harmonic tremor.

One bee at the tip
Of a nettle, settled at work.
And then another and another…

There is no nest, only the swarm
At work on resin—the tree's voicebox sings—
The tree stretches up, expanded vocal chords in the throat of the eye.
The tree hums one extended, braided, unbreakable note.

§
Skin's wing, wing, wing, wing:
Sings blue sky into roots,
Sings myna birds onto a nearby fence post.
Sings ohia roots
Deep in the a'a'.
Sings El Camino chasing Two Color
Up a pasture road toward the volcano.
The sound of the bees takes the shape
Of the sound the trees would make
If I was not me.
Sings me away until I am nothing
But the memory of a mongoose stalking a bird.
Until I am nothing but the surface
Of my skin, and a hum.
Skin's wing, wing, wing, wing.

DELTA 14: ON OUR LAST WALK PAST THE EDGE OF THE NEIGHBORHOOD I NOTICED A MAN PATCHING HIS FENCE

I'm in Orlando, the magic kingdom of every thing.
Magic tricks God out of taking what can't be remembered
As boredom's least expected twin sister. Please read
While listening to Madame Gandhi's "Yellow Sea."
The magician reveals a piece of you you didn't know was there.
One of the most beautiful tricks of fall? Late blooming
Blue-eyed grass. The "Yellow Sea" is three minutes and forty-one
Seconds long; this poem will take about three minutes and forty-one
Seconds to read. My bus ride to the Hotel Coronado
Has come to an end. Just a few days ago, Bay and I were driving
Through a eucalyptus forest. Inhale: eucalyptus, yes?
On our last walk past the edge of the neighborhood,
Bay was telling me about the day without Mr. B,
The day the substitute didn't get anything done.
Bay said, "Lindsey's dads are the class moms. They helped.
Ritee pushed Leonid. Soo ate Malik's cookie. Ishmael
And Prakash hid Ali's homework. Elham kissed Rashad.
Alvarez and Quyaan killed Alvey, the albino praying mantis,
Our class pet. Zeus' moms handed out not-good cupcakes."
I noticed a man patching his fence. I said, I thought, in jest,
"Hey, you have a hole in your fence," intending to strike up
A conversation. The sword swallows a roll of dimes.
We hear, "What an asshole. What the hell is your problem?
Who the hell do you think you are?" Better fences?
He walked after us. I walked back towards him,
Wanting to apologize
And to confront him.
A pink-eyed rabbit juggles a dozen top hats.
Half an assistant glues a volunteer to heather.
A fish picks the lock. If a curtain hypnotized the pulley
Then the clouds below would have no sky beneath them.
Four linked doves pull a handkerchief over the guillotine.

The just finished storm leaks across the sidewalk. The campus
Air dabbed with varietals from a palette of petrichor.
A head has feet for ears until vice has a last drink
Of absinthe. A wand pours bottle after bottle
Into a pile of rope. The levitating hourglass takes a bow, signs
Autographs in cursive repeating the same expression,
"You wear me out, you wear me out, you wear me out."
From the back of the audience to the street. I am burning alive
Inside an apple missed by an arrow shot from the eyes
Of John's horse. The rope next to the chain link fence climbs
Aboard. I swallowed a pack of razor blades. Here's yours.
We have learned to love the lively impact of sulfur when we cross
The San Mateo Bridge. Sulfur. As I write this in the Coronado hotel
In Orlando I imagine Bay at home eating pizza at the counter,
The yeastiness slick in the cool air. (A few hours after writing this
I learn he was eating spaghetti & meatballs.)
The TV is on; the puppy monkey baby
Mountain Dew commercial has him laughing.
A childhood friend's friend's card is the garden
Shovel of hearts. Inside the ear of corn a finch found
A stack of white gloves — all left hands.
Who is the keynote speaker? Michelle Obama.
Touch the mark's hand: on the peak
Of the mountain ridge of one range of your fingerprint
There is a moment happening. A sleight of hand, shown, given,
Believed, burned away. Now you feel the low tide
That exposes the sandbar and the muddy shoals.
TaskRabbit your dirty laundry. You won't miss it if you blink.
The ball tells the shill the right card lost its mind to the middle cup.
Close your eyes, think of a pony, any pony. Blue-eyed grass
Will return. A bullet drops a set of false teeth from the floor
Of an invisible cabinet. He turned the corner
And did not let me look him in the eye.

SCATTERPLOT: SUPERMAN BATTLES CTHULHU UNDER THE WATCHFUL EYE OF THE ZAP-GUN

Consider the boy in his brown cap at the aquarium
Watching a water column's rising pockets of air
Like unnamed UFOs through the phosphor.
Consider the net his mind makes of the blonde
Naso tang, an arrowed school of blue hippo
Tang, a vertical flight of raccoon butterfly.
Consider he has no words for their arrays
Of saffron and turquoise encoded in his chamber,
Image before name surfaces on delight's tongue.
Consider the blessing and the curse when the guide
Points a finger, like a strange Michelangelic god
Backlit by aquarium blue, and says, "The blonde naso tang"
Points again, "blue hippo tang" and points again,
"Raccoon butterfly," beautiful breathing something
Something's named, snipped from the nameless.
Consider Philip K. Dick's zap-gun defending,
Destroying, rebuilding, defending and further destroying
And defending without. Without what, David?
Without thinking about the otherwise, a memory
Of my father holding my son connecting "water"
To water: the electron in the wire, for so long
Unknowable and unseen, then knowable and unseen,
Then seen, and now unknowable and unseeable.
Consider the distant smoke threatening with new fire.
The floating island of a brown cap hides
A crystal ball where Superman battles Cthulu
Under the watchful eye of the zap-gun.

FROM CATULLUS: FOURTEEN ERASURES FROM THE LATIN OF THE LAST THREE LINES OF CARMEN 48 BASED ON AN EXERCISE FROM REBECCA RESINSKI

name a turf used to

    equate no arid regions

a rat's ass is not rain

am I fun or a rose's goat?

murder is art is not a soul

    (cum, quiet, ode, sadness)

dear future, art is not rage,

osculation is

    endears, or egos, us

a video's dense gel is

    Saturn on siege, SOS, OS …

am I a turn or a session?

    equations see us

DELTA 15: THE DEFINITION OF A CIRCLE IN A WORLD WITHOUT GEOMETRY

The Rycoff's have planted blood-red batface along the edge of the walk.
They will get all the hummingbirds and butterflies
Next year. Push play. Of course I have to mention how my mind
Does not want to mention
This entire night, underscored by Wilco's lines
"I'd always thought that if I held you tightly
You'd always love me like you did back then"
Omits, as Mayakovsky would call her, the target.
My son, Bay and I, walk past Thing 1 and Thing 2.
How many ballerinas does one expect to see
Walking the streets this late at night?
Death is always on the prowl: the near miss of Rusty
By the Home Depot truck in New York City
Brings the near misses back today:
My idea of the soul is a dance party with palm trees
Wrapped in foil. Dancing is flying and the music
Always sounds like the first time you heard the Talking Heads
Combined with the second time you listened to Velvet Underground's
Self-titled album all the way through.
My third eye takes naps. Nods off without warning.
Right now, I am asleep with two eyes open.
The hunchback of Notre Dame answers the door of the house
At the corner of Harbor Cove and River. The inmate, in his prison
Stripes, holds his one-year-old son, also in prison stripes.
The scantily clad prison guard swings her billy club.
Oh, never to be stuck in commute traffic again.
We all learn, eventually, "don't read the comments."
Minions have taken over the neighborhood.
A witch doused in gauze cackles
From her corner of the walkway; a skeleton sits on our bench
Doing its best impression of William Logan, right leg
Crossed over left, right arm stretched out to the right, skull
Tilted to 11, chin and right toe pointed to 4.

A bottle of hand sanitizer, almost empty, cranes its neck
Over the edge of the second edition unabridged <u>Webster's</u>
<u>New International Dictionary</u>, 1958.
Paul Manafort walks by dressed up as a train engineer.
The Rycoff family, dressed as the knights of the round table,
Ring the doorbell of the largest house in the neighborhood.
The head of the HOA, a former porn star, shows up at the party
As a 2007 IRS tax audit of Jeff Sessions. A guy with a bonfire
Wheel in his driveway hands out Heinekens. Push stop.
The definition of a circle in a world without geometry
Sources its etymology from the fleeing prisoner, innocent
Despite all the charges, born in Cande, France, a short drive
From the College du Combree where he learned
How to love an older woman. Where she and her sister
Took him after the school day was over, but time allowed.
"Never trust the living," said Juno, played by Sylvia Sidney, in <u>Beetlejuice</u>.
The line, a set of lines, intersecting Sumi lines, outline
The idea of the face of a ram, ink drops like mistakes, like eyes,
Like the image of planets in a solar system, like orbits,
Like the beginning moment that determines the weight of a line:
Samhain, the stray red balloon, the "somebody start something."
I dressed as a wolfman, Bay, a wolfboy. We howl because we howl.
The root of how the moon turns us. The skeleton in the red shawl
Escorts us to the courtyard. There in the 18th card, an owl in the tree
Sees two wolves calling down the partial moon.
There in the distance, the Sierras wait all winter.
A mastiff dressed in a tuxedo walks by, pauses.

SCATTERPLOT: ESSAY ON GRANITE

Set the chin, the hearth, the mantle, the rock garden:
Ground the house in place with us as polished, masoned,
Beveled, fitted. Even the children handmade, yet,
If anything, we share the fingertip's cobbled-peppery
Sense of granite's composite oneness. The bedrock
For the arbor near the sculpture garden: paperweight,
Glacial medium. Chiselers thread dates because written
In stone means someone cared for life near the lake's
Edge. Jointed scarps make rock climbing seem required.
The fixedness of things, power, the reminder
That no oppressor, only fluid stone, will endure.
In this story someone fell and splattered on the stones
Of a V-shaped gorge.   Hardness
Just malleable enough to be shaped matters most.

SCATTERPLOT: YOSEMITE LOSTNESS FABLE

I mistake the walking stick for something numinous. I divine rod the
    nomenclature. Yet no amount of falls in the distance.
If stars, ignoring the obvious in order to stay calm comes at a discount. What
    would happen if you were found with your pants
Down. Sunrise picks a direction for the day, all day, once a day. Uphill rivers
    run away toward undesired rescues.
The oulets walk underwater, mine began as an algebra that became arithmetic
    where both sides of the equator could not rotate.
Dead cell, a life endurance policy rattles in the rock box. A winged thing
    extending risk to the edge of the fall. I began
Again as. I began again as wind as in find. His began again as Cimon and
    Pero, the strangeness of an adult
Stepdaughter's unbroken. How cataracts and iris bows, how foam-washed
    bosses, how one man's lostness. I am Grimm failure, so I
Might never leave the meadow, so that my children might starve because their
    voices have closed their throats up, so that gingerbread days,
So that forever flightless escape from. I made myself compass, degree, ascend,
    track, summit, repel. My body of work
Is an unreliable thing. My body rappels. Grope Cimon, grope true north, the
    handspring, the string of throng, waver curves,
Arched back of buttress, unreachable bridge uncrossed by fingers threading the
    hold. If I let go? She lets go. Pursue dashing,
Surge, wet granite slurs the air with call. Choice, a fan-shaped thing, and
    returns are a gentian not happenstance yearning. If I could only
Give up. Demi-sun, demi-shade, wild doublings, the mange. Flame-shaped,
    spring grass brown black bear, glint off telescopic lens looking out mis-
Leads me in. My body never agains.

SCATTERPLOT: ODE TO A BROKEN TYPEWRITER FOUND WHILE HIKING WITH MY SON (PICARESQUE)

As I scramble up an unmarked trail
Edged with decomposed granite, I think
Of a screaming tea kettle. Where you
Slope in spring you weep. I have never
Been to Prague. John Muir has never
Been to Prague. My neighbor's uncle Bob,
As far as I know, has never been
To Prague. No one wants to know the truth.
The typewriter I found and carry
With me in my hands insists I name
This ode, "Ode to Altitude Sickness"
or "Ode to the Tuolumne County
Facts from the US Census Bureau."
4% of Tuolumne County
Is under 5 years of age compared
To 10% from across the state.
This suggests they sacrifice their young.
In Prague I made love to a lovely
Horse with a flaxen mane. Your zipper
Is down. Water funnels occur here
Infrequently. Atop the rise I
Will be unable to say anything
But "oh my, oh my." This means I am
Thinking about beauty or about
How many children have been pushed
To their death by mentally ill
Parents. Prague is populated
With lovely horses. Water, water,
Water. Near the top, I consider
Re-typing the title of this ode
But the typewriter says, "That would not
Make sense, so if you meant that I
Think that's super." A raisin is stuck

In my front teeth, the typewriter calls
The pinkish petal in the burrow
Of my face a boatman's tongue. Evening's
Flares catch a peregrine falcon
At speed, shoulders back, targeting fish
In Lake Tenaya. The typewriter
Tells us the story about the chief
The lake is named for, his brutal
Murder at the hands of his fellow
Gamblers. The peregrine can't fly
Higher than 17 feet above
The lake with a catch of that size. Mist,
More concentrated than Bruce Lee's sweat,
Murders everything. At this point
I am considering renaming
This ode to "Odious Ode." Or "Ode
To the Red Garbage Can by My Desk."
Do not trust the handmaids of Prague.
Do not trust the handmaids of Prague!
They are both missing a syllable!
A broken typewriter is a sad thing.
On the descent with horsetail light watch
Me endure the ending. The "broken
Back of an aging stegosaurus,"
He says. Miscalculated in scale,
I think. The typewriter keys have jammed
Their consonants and punctuation
Into each other's backs. We vowel
The vowels. Tea leaves left to molder
In morning's kitchen. Dog Lake will not fetch.
The horse of my Prague goes it alone.
XYZPDQ. Honeybees
Do not trust a bloom when the promise breaks.
Fuck the gods. Fuck madness. I never
Want to die. Only undeserving
Gods would call for fathers to give up
Their sons for something other than this.

DELTA 17: SLOUGH WATER NEVER SO CLEAR AS FLOW TIDE IN NOVEMBER

The charade: peace sign, make a fist and circle
It over your ear while looking through the fist
On your other hand with your right eye open
And left eye closed, next pinch the thumb
On the left hand with your thumb and forefinger
In your right and pull them apart, run in place.
I should be erasing Sherlock Holmes for Rebecca.
Instead, the coyote scat, the dead field
Mouse covered in flies, the stump of a eucalyptus
Tree, a rectangular sheet of plywood seesaws
In the ripples: we hope for a monster. A silver's pink
Caudal fin tapers the surface with ribbon.
My daughter, Anna, home for Thanksgiving,
Works to unbreak our hearts. Ahead of me,
She walks past an orange cone with a broom handle
Stuck down its throat, a broken built-in sprinkler spouts off.
The ice maker spits ice cubes
On the floor for the dog to chew. Beyond us a blue heron
And a white egret prop themselves atop water
Hyacinth. In "It's Everyday Bro" Gucci insists
"In 1997, I would pull up in a Buick."
Someone taps the open mouth of the foil
Coffee bag against the back of their hand shaking
Free the last grounds. Thanksgiving
Was but a handful of menu items 20 years ago.
Last night we constructed a periodic table of mints:
From Horehound to Tic Tacs to Pimentos.
Today the baroque menu includes over 30.
Each year a new dish. She says, "A pack of coyotes
Chased me. I was out for a morning run,
Training for the 10k I want to do with Tress."
She pockets her hands. "At first, I was like,
Whatever, a couple of dogs, no big deal."

Persimmon pie: blend coconut milk,
Fresh persimmons, a touch of pumpkin pie
Spice, and maple syrup. This year's bibelot.
A neighbor posted a picture of a western
Black widow in their mailbox. Anemic
Since she was a child, she bruises easily.
She says the black and white photo of Muhammad Ali
Punching the Beatles should sit atop the years
Of Omnidawn not the spy novels below
The picture of the older kids and I
Surfing the beach break in Pismo. I highlight
In yellow the word "lithotype." We smoked
The duck over low heat. You are the desperate search
Of a USB adapter for an iPhone charger.
You are the ten-pack of reading glasses from Walgreens.
My middle finger on a hospital bed dreams
In the sound quality of AM radio.
I have 337 Neanderthal variants:
"This is more than 99% of 23andMe Customers."
Anna left the Bay Area to go live with her mother.
Her grandfather wears golf shoes
In the house. Rebecca highlighted the word "footstep."
Note: the crackle of a chocolate covered
Espresso bean between molars purchases
A moment away from the whispers behind the wall,
The shampoo commercial on the flat screen, the pre-occupation
Of what's taking so long from everything taking so long.
Widow spiders eat the heads of their mates
And so do not belong to our class of monsters.
The swamp thing, the giant ant, the sharktopus: manifestations
Of what flits the lips of the aging musician's smile.
Feed the milk a cup of scribbled cat.
The baitfish in the slough angle into the reflections.

SCATTERPLOT: IN LIMBO AT THE MILLENNIUM

And at what cost this mirrored spire? A jar
Of Mauna Loa nuts mirrored over a mahogany

Desk like a bachelor party joke for the groom…
Pinheads of New York's pedestrians represent

Themselves from halfway points this high up.
Just another business trip to NYC.

Not thinking of you, again. A salesman dines
With me at Patsy's. I feel so small at Sinatra's

Feet I can't eat much. Just a clef note
In the larger jumble. All around me, what hokum!

The dishes clatter with the repressed eagerness
Of the chef's voice then muted after a glass breaks.

Sometimes stewardesses from The Millennium
Carry me away from the trappings of this business.

They work hard to help, knowing, we're "here today,
Gone tomorrow." Their faces never so young

As when reflected in the still pond of a martini.
On the pillow, there is a note from The Millennium

Welcoming me. In the desk, there is a postcard
Of the hotel overseeing the Statue of Liberty.

Another with a smiling showgirl, all bird of paradise,
And neon, flush lips plump with expectation.

SCATTERPLOT: NOOSE

Why are contracts with God the easiest to break?
I've seen the flats of Flamingo take the shape of tide and come

To understand that at flood there is little to be. The first
Front door swings closed for the last time in a memory

Too young to remember. Every sewer grate is labeled with the name
Of my birth town. What you thought of her hair laced

With the tatting of the diner's air. The prayer was a prayer
For self and a contract with god that would not be kept.

What you heard from the sidewalk outside of the Warfield
After the latest band has left the stage. The meditation

Was in a man concerned with those he did not know.
I've heard the ebb take the shape of time and the redfish

At work on minnows. The front doors of Versailles are not
The front doors of Versailles or else all doors are the front doors

Of Versailles. Every birth is a reminder of his failures.
What the light hid from the boy's face lit by the candlelight

Of a cell phone. The prayer was for my son that I would not have
But for asking of a god for what I did not believe in. Maybe I

Steadied the boat staid by mud where once there was water.
The door of the hospital room swung open, the room flooded

With a school of nurses. In that prayer, the noose was loosened,
The umbilical knot untied, and unsettled sea, settled.

SCATTERPLOT: SHADOW THIEF

Do not wonder why he was not postage stamp maker, filmmaker, or mortician. Not Rorschach test, not symptom of pareidolia, not haunting, he sidesteps and turns. (His daydream of Joseph Cornell premiering <u>Rose Hobart</u>, the inflamed Salvador Dali knocking the camera to the floor because Cornell had stolen the picture from his subconscious, distracts him from the task at hand.)

The projectionist knows exactly the light he likes, light gray at the edges, light flickering with hesitation as if illumination itself were worn out: the essential quality of a former self—light, to him, like God's. Night's window catches him praying, his umbra (the blackest part of a shadow from which all light is cut off) a distinct torso.

You happen when he steals the music box—silver edging, brass-tacked leather, tongue clasp snapped in lock's dark latch—off the mantle. Opened. Around the dancer's spinning legs orbits a tin ring—all dusk, through a tall corridor, a blind alley follows the thief home. Her paint, pale and worn but for the tiny dashes of where he touched-up her red lips.

DELTA 19: IF YOU WERE GIVEN A SELF-DRIVING CAR, WHAT WOULD YOU DO WITH IT?

The dying world—we eradicate the mosquitoes
And kill off the dragonflies.
A conversation between Anna, my daughter, and I? We are a dying breed:
Pest Control has swept through the community and no memory
Of wrestling on the carpet in the middle
Of the family room can save
Us from her mother, head in hands, saying, "She's going to get hurt,
She's going to get hurt, she's going to get hurt, she's going to get hurt."
In the attic, the Greek chorus tramples
Over the hobby horse and half-full cardboard boxes.
Push your Tile and the misplaced iPad rings from the laundry room.
The outcome of Stage 1 is to get to Stage 2. This is how we talk.
The parallelogram of the razorblade signals the season.
The crumpled ball of yellowed paper with the orange lightning bolt
Drawn on it rests in the arms of the bronze Kraken. When younger
We talked about not staying when
You are the lover but need to be the loved.
In the delta even the rivers have tides.
There is no form in the pressure within the fault.
If you were given a self-driving car, what would you do with it?
"U.S. House approves sweeping tax bill in a win for Trump."
The divorce papers issued song lines for the caribou migration
Where the splayed hoof has adapted
To walking where others get stuck.
As you pass by the Sacramento, an olive tree exhales a henhouse.
Notice if you look left when looking for source, this means you look
Away from the right of the office: a knot in the back tilts the world
Towards the singing.
Rainbow Kitten Surprise croons "The times
That we believed in a cocaine Jesus in a black four-seater…"
When our misspent youth spread rumors about the need to need
You have a lover you would love right now if they called.
As a child at the farmers market

Anna pushed the seed
Into the loam, sprayed the surface with water. Forgotten
In the backyard, the years lined with deer tongue.

SCATTERPLOT: PORTRAIT OF THE ARTIST AS A PLAYLIST SONNET

"I Wanna Rock n Roll All Night," "Kiss" "The Wild Women of Wongo,"
"Burn," "Down by the River," "Once" "We Are All On Drugs"
"Playing God" "Upside Down" "Undone." "With Her Head Underneath
Her Arm" "Into Her" "Near Death Experience Experience," "All I Know"
"Next Year" "You'll Be Mine," "Because," "Ugly," "You'll
Always Be Beautiful," "Be Like That" "Ziggy Stardust" "Song
On the Radio." "You Must Be Bleeding Under Your Eyelids."
"Admit It." "Admit It Again" "You Are" "Stoned." "Yes" "This Is It"
"A Perfect Day," "All the Things That I Have Done." "Amanda,"
"Please Don't Let Me Go." "Can You Read My Mind," "Amanda?"
"I Wanna Rock n Roll All Night," "Kiss" "The Wild Women of Wongo."
"Amanda," "Can't You See" "I Like What You Say." "Everything
You Say," "F--K Yeah," "Flowers" "Into Dust." "I Never Told You
What I Do For A Living." "I've Discovered" "You're Gonna Live Forever (In Me)."

SCATTERPLOT: MORNING MEDITATION BUSTED SONNET SEQUENCE FAILURE 19

Passport renewal, driver license renewal, 59
Emails in a must-do list from last week. Make sure red
Illuminati t-shirt gets into the washing machine for tomorrow
Night's event. Remove mole above left eye. Remove I.
Don't forget to eat berries with granola. Say: remember to eat
Berries with granola. Tell Michael to read George Oppen.
Call Andrew. Rollover IRA. Don't get drunk. Say: Just for today.
Get to a meeting. Remind hollowness to de-bird her bones.
Remind bones to re-bird hollowness. Andre Iguodala, yeah baby!
100,000-mile tune-up, repair dents in body, prostate exam.
Does car really need repair? Prepare quarterly business review.
Prepare tasting menu on letterpress. Snarf, pickle, custard.
Don't die. Say: live. Remember cushion, anus, ball sack,
Thighs, shins, calves, ankles, feet. I wonder who else
Considers their genitals public…meaning not private or social.
I like the idea of social genitals. You know, AC/DC,
"…some balls are held for charity / and some for fancy dress…"
No? Really? I need coffee. Opens in 19 minutes. Don't look
At the time. Say: stay with the breath. Could use a smoke.
But we agreed I don't smoke. Pay gardener, pay tuitions, pay
Health club, mortgage, electric, gas, car, daycare, violin teacher,
Visa, taxes, the piper. Ask handsome to history sum
Multiplication for nary a self-parody lacks one. Ask handsome
To press advice into their intercourse. Donate, check-in, give
Away, repair, fix, find, disrupt, schedule, invest, contribute,
Write, submit, cook, eat, clean, pick up, drop off, maintain,
Upgrade, download, convince, argue, dissuade, advise,
Explain, coerce, discuss, lurch, stub, stumble, gripe, grope,
Group, go. Don't forget to love. Say: love.

DELTA 20: CROSSING THE BRIDGE TO TASSAJARA TRAIL

The pool's LEDs whisper blue light.
Dark marble crickets walk the concrete looking
For a way to water. A dozen or more types live in our fields
Singing their discretions. The torn and frayed dirt split by drought
Hides them and their impending invasion in the next thunderstorm,
Their gods, ushering them out in force. I rub my forewings and sing:
This year's months were the odors of the children born in them.
"Four children. A dog. A little ray of sun. The 96. It is two o'clock."
With 120 to collect I include here the taxonomic guide
Of the seven arcana from Astro Mutants to Evil Zomboidz.
The speed of my traveling has slowed from road trips to walks.
I have not yet disassembled my composer's needle and thread.
My father always said the people closest to you will like you least.
My contour of Perec's An Attempt at Exhausting a Place in Paris
On display: how I fail as a father, as a lover, as a lifeguard.
You are addicted to the idea
That you are different and this is the source of the affliction:
To disagree and remain in conflict as intensely toward nuance
As toward murder lifts your spirits. The tangle of cords
To power your devices—your planned obsolescence—
Looks exactly like mine. You will not be in the book.
You can listen to Kele Okereke's drop dead Current Inspiration
Playlist and you may find Sleater-Kinney's "Start Together"
Or you may not, because "Right or wrong, here we are."
This is where we insert a wall made of revolving doors.
The east end of the desk's dark wood, waves jammed
With yellow post-its noted asymmetrically with Sharpie thoughts,
There the memory of Bay looking back over his left shoulder
While crossing the re-built walking bridge, the dry creek under,
To the midpoint of Tassajara Trail.
Sometimes 11 point font
Seems smaller than it should be as if it were typed on paper
A day prior and reached the mind a day later.
The way the seed of the California lotus changes color

To match the local dirt.
In spring the imbalanced fingernail-leafed
Stems and yellow mantis-faced flowers seem unremarkable
And at once suddenly everywhere.
The people closest to you still want to know the least about you.
The psychologists say a common fear of the mad
Is that all nutritional value has been removed from food
Which does not seem so mad.
Julie asked the question: "What happens when
You can go no further and you go further?"
I have invented a way to hide my start in the dirt wherever I love.
To know how people have lived ask for their level of expertise
With a heavy duty handheld tape dispenser.
I feel the loss of my mind approaching.
I just tried to put a pair of reading
Glasses on top of the pair of reading glasses I am wearing.
I just wrote, "Bay watching I Love Lucy on Christmas Eve
Reminds me of his dead grandmother." He walks into my office,
Looks over my shoulder, he asks, "Whatcha doing? Writing a poem?
What's it about?" I tilt the face of the laptop
Down embarrassed by the line. I delete the line and say
"I'm working Mutant Mania into it."
We just inventoried Mutant Mania. Rebuilt Dr. Decay:
The leg and foot in his left hand, the surgery blade in his right,
Purple shorts and a teal polo. Brain exposed above his headlight
And the lovely forever
Of black pupils in the yellow half-moons of his eyes.
The children were a pile of receipts from 1990 lit on fire and smoked.
The fire was a candle flame in a Moroccan holder at the far end of a hall
Where the last person through left behind a tumbler of melting ice.
Bay thinks we should also tell you about Body Slam Bat.
His grey wrestling boots at the end of his pink legs bowing
Out from his teal leotard. His royal blue wings match his ears,
Ears the size of his head. The six sets of fangs in a mouth
That runs ear to ear rival for attention the tiny black dots
Within the lime green arcs of his proptosic eyeballs.
Such toys don't quite restore faith, the names used to describe

The character reveal the character and yet only closer inspection
Of their expression or what they wear or how they are shaped
Disclose the subtle array of powers at their disposal. To spend
Time as we do, looking so closely at something but an inch tall
Tells me that within we see each other not in the eyes we share
But in the mind moving over the tentacled head of Shocktopus
Or petting the array of T-wrecker's Mohawk.
The streetlight beyond the frame in a picture of seven satellite dishes
At the entrance of an apartment complex in Miami, Florida
Casts seven swollen shadows on the stucco veneer.
The curtain covered windows whisper something about their hue.
Green, green grass, even at night, betrays the soil's water table.
Tells the story of how the lawn parts to make room for the walkway.
I read in a poem that the mad fear they cannot close doors,
Doors refuse to close.
This does not seem so mad.
Inside several tenants are late on their rent. A respirator clicks
And lapses keeping the owner of the building alive, her daughter
Sits at her bedside in New Jersey General reading a dime store novel:
"The wife loved her husband deeply and could not imagine her life
Without him, so she saw no other way but to kill him while he slept."
The wind has scattered us everywhere, we sing down lightning.

David's first chapbook *Coil* (University of Alaska, 1998), won the Midnight Sun Chapbook Contest. His first full-length manuscript, *Twine* (Bauhan Publishing, 2013), won the May Sarton Poetry Prize. David co-edited *Compendium*, (Omnidawn Publishing, 2017), a text offering Donald Justice's original syllabus on prosody. David holds an MFA from the University of Florida, a Bachelors in Creative Writing from Carnegie Mellon, an M.Ed (TFA) from the University of Alaska. David's writing appears in a range of magazines including *Prairie Schooner*, *Gargoyle*, *Hotel Amerika*, *Kenyon Review*, *New England Review*, *Alaska Quarterly Review*, *Volt*, *Carolina Quarterly*, *Diagram*, *McSweeney's*, *The Greensboro Review*, *North American Review*, and many others.

Scatterplot
by David Koehn

Cover art:
Tucker Nichols, *Untitled (PA1903)*, 2019
10" x 8", paint on panel

Cover typeface: Avenir LT Std
Interior typeface: Adobe Caslon Pro

Cover & interior design by Cassandra Smith

Printed in the United States
by Books International, Dulles, Virginia
On 55# Glatfelter B19 Antique
Acid Free Archival Quality Recycled Paper

Publication of this book was made possible in part by gifts from
Katherine & John Gravendyk in honor of Hillary Gravendyk,
Francesca Bell, Mary Mackey, and The New Place Fund

Omnidawn Publishing
Oakland, California
Staff and Volunteers, Spring 2020

Rusty Morrison & Ken Keegan, senior editors & co-publishers
Kayla Ellenbecker, production editor
Gillian Olivia Blythe Hamel, senior editor & book designer
Trisha Peck, senior editor & book designer
Rob Hendricks, marketing assistant & *Omniverse* editor
Cassandra Smith, poetry editor & book designer
Sharon Zetter, poetry editor & book designer
Liza Flum, poetry editor
Matthew Bowie, poetry editor
Juliana Paslay, fiction editor
Gail Aronson, fiction editor
Izabella Santana, fiction editor & marketing assistant
SD Sumner, copyeditor